BLACK AMERICANS OF DISTINCTION

IMPORTANT BLACK AMERICANS IN
Civil Rights and Politics

Stephen Currie

ReferencePoint
Press®

San Diego, CA

ReferencePoint
Press®

© 2023 ReferencePoint Press, Inc.
Printed in the United States

For more information, contact:
ReferencePoint Press, Inc.
PO Box 27779
San Diego, CA 92198
www.ReferencePointPress.com

LIBRARY OF CONGRESS CATALOGING-IN-PUBLICATION DATA

Names: Currie, Stephen, 1960- author.
Title: Important Black Americans in civil rights and politics / by Stephen Currie.
Description: San Diego, CA : ReferencePoint Press, Inc., 2023. | Series:
  Black Americans of distinction | Includes bibliographical references and index.
Identifiers: LCCN 2021051262 (print) | LCCN 2021051263 (ebook) | ISBN
  9781678202866 (library binding) | ISBN 9781678202873 (ebook)
Subjects: LCSH: African American politicians--Biography--Juvenile
  literature. | African American political activists--Biography--Juvenile
  literature. | African American civil rights workers--Biography--Juvenile
  literature. | African Americans--Politics and government--Juvenile
  literature. | African Americans--Civil rights--Juvenile literature.
Classification: LCC E185.96 .C87 2023 (print) | LCC E185.96 (ebook) | DDC
  920.0092/96073--dc23/eng/20220310
LC record available at https://lccn.loc.gov/2021051262
LC ebook record available at https://lccn.loc.gov/2021051263

CONTENTS

Activism and Government

The United States in the early twentieth century was an unjust and often dangerous place for Black Americans. In many parts of the country, laws and customs worked together to keep Black people from fully participating in society. Part of the problem was segregation, or division of the races. Until 1968 segregation was the law in many states. Segregation ensured that African Americans could not live in certain communities, were forced to attend underfunded schools for Blacks only, and were forbidden from using seating areas, waiting rooms, and even water fountains designated for the use of Whites. In addition to suffering under these harsh laws, Blacks typically had few financial resources, lacked basic freedoms such as the right to vote, and were treated as social inferiors by Whites.

Many Blacks and some northern Whites did not tolerate these unfair policies and fought for social and legal equality for all Americans. The years following the end of World War II in 1945 saw the rise of the civil rights movement, an effort launched by African Americans to claim the rights that are supposed to be granted to everyone. By the 1950s this movement was well under way. Protesters held peaceful rallies to present their list of demands: racial integration in schools and elsewhere, the right to vote, and just and respectful treatment in society.

In most cases, however, the protests did not immediately lead to change. On the contrary, enraged White people—typically in southern states, where segregation was the law—often attacked the activists. Peaceful protesters were sprayed with fire hoses, beaten by citizens and police officers, and in a few cases killed.

Still, the civil rights movement made headway. A boycott in Montgomery, Alabama, for example, led to the end of segregated seating on that city's buses. A 1954 Supreme Court decision invalidated legal segregation in public schools. Courageous Black men and women registered to vote and showed up at the polls despite threats of violence. The civil rights movement was not successful in everything it did. In some areas the laws changed, but enforcement was lax and threats remained. Today racism continues to be a major problem in the United States, and Whites still outpace Blacks in almost every quality-of-life measure. But the movement played a major role in making the country a better place.

Leaders

The most famous civil rights leader was Dr. Martin Luther King Jr., an Atlanta, Georgia, preacher who served in many ways as the moral center of the movement and was perhaps the leading proponent of nonviolence. But King was by no means the only leader of the movement. Fannie Lou Hamer worked tirelessly to give Black people voting rights in Mississippi and elsewhere; she became known for her rallying cry, "I am sick and tired of being sick and tired."[1] Rosa Parks sparked the Montgomery bus boycott by refusing to yield her seat to a White passenger when instructed to do so by a White bus driver. Ralph Abernathy, John Lewis, and Medgar Evers were instrumental in planning and leading protests. And thousands of others were active in the movement as well, from children integrating public schools to demonstrators risking their lives to fight for their rights.

> "I am sick and tired of being sick and tired."[1]
>
> —Fannie Lou Hamer, civil rights activist

The marches and protests of the civil rights movement have always attracted the most attention. But even in the 1950s and 1960s, many African Americans fought for civil rights through politics and the law. Black lawyer Thurgood Marshall argued the famous *Brown v. Board of Education* case that ended legal segregation in the public schools. African Americans Barbara Jordan, Adam Clayton Powell, and Shirley Chisholm were congressional leaders during the civil rights era. Chisholm, a New York Demo-

The most famous civil rights leader was Dr. Martin Luther King Jr. (pictured). King served in many ways as the moral center of the movement and was perhaps the leading proponent of nonviolent protesting.

crat, actually ran for her party's nomination for president in 1972, saying that she wanted to "demonstrate the sheer will and refusal to accept the status quo."[2]

More recently, the number of African American government leaders has increased. Barack Obama became president in 2009, and Kamala Harris was elected vice president in 2020. As of 2021 three US senators were Black, two of them from states in the Deep South. Condoleezza Rice and Colin Powell (who died in October 2021 at the age of eighty-four) both served as secretary of state under former president George W. Bush; Lloyd Austin serves as secretary of defense under current president Joe Biden. Not all of these people have taken part in the political struggle for civil rights legislation, but many have. Harris was an early supporter of marriage equality; political strategist and former member of the Georgia House of Representatives Stacey Abrams has focused on ensuring the right to vote.

This is not to say that the protests of the 1950s and 1960s are gone. They are not, as the rise of Black Lives Matter and similar groups in the twenty-first century shows. But African Americans in politics demonstrate that change can be brought about through government policy and law as well as through marches and demonstrations. Neither approach has a monopoly on effectiveness. Many of the improvements to African American lives over the years have been the result of a combination of the two. That will surely continue to be the case in the future as well.

CHAPTER ONE

Thurgood Marshall: Lawyer and Supreme Court Justice

The law has not often been friendly to Black Americans. The US Constitution, after all, originally gave states the power to make Black slavery legal, and many states did exactly that. Later, laws limited where African Americans could live and work. The segregation of schools by race was perfectly legal, even required, in many places; other laws required that Blacks sit separately from Whites in movie theaters, on buses, and in waiting rooms. Yet many civil rights activists have looked to the law as a way to ensure better treatment for African Americans. These leaders focused on changing laws to make them inclusive of Blacks rather than excluding them; they worked to make the legal system one that matched morality rather than mocking it. Foremost among these leaders was the first African American on the Supreme Court, a man named Thurgood Marshall.

Childhood Through College

Born in 1908, Thurgood Marshall grew up in Baltimore, Maryland. His mother was a teacher at a local school for Black children; his father worked as a railroad porter and then as a steward at an all-White yacht club. These positions not only paid reasonably well for the time, but they provided a degree of status and job security as well. By the standards of Baltimore's Black community, the Marshalls were comfortably middle class. Still, the family was aware of the racism prevalent in daily life. Thurgood's father advised him that if anyone called him offensive names, "you not only got my permission to fight him—you got my orders to fight him."[3]

In 1925 Marshall graduated from high school and went on to further study at all-Black Lincoln University in Pennsylvania. To pay his tuition, he held a succession of jobs, including baker and grocery store clerk. At Lincoln he excelled in debate but was not a particularly strong student. Marshall had a reputation on campus as a practical joker, and he was suspended at least twice for breaking college rules. Not until late in his college career did Marshall begin studying seriously. By this time he had made two important life decisions. First, he had gotten married to a student named Vivien Burey. Second, he had decided to become a lawyer.

The next step for Marshall should have been to attend the law school at the University of Maryland in his home state. But the college itself was segregated, and the law school had a policy of not admitting African American students at all. Barred from Maryland's law school because of his race, Marshall opted instead to attend the school of law at Howard University, a historically Black institution in Washington, DC. There, he studied harder than ever, and his hard work paid off. In 1933 he graduated first in his class and returned to Baltimore to open his own law office.

Marshall and the NAACP

At Lincoln, Marshall had not been particularly active in the struggle for civil rights. Indeed, he spoke against student agitation to hire African American professors (when he began college, the entire faculty at the university was White), leading one classmate to describe Marshall as "loud and wrong."[4] Being kept out of the University of Maryland's law school changed his outlook, however. Marshall would devote most of his future legal practice to civil rights work, even though many of his clients could not pay.

By 1936, writes author James Poling, Marshall had "built up the largest law practice in Baltimore and still couldn't pay his rent."[5]

From early in his legal career, Marshall worked extensively with the National Association for the Advancement of Colored People (NAACP), a civil rights organization founded in 1909. One of his first cases with the organization involved a Black man named Donald Murray, who went to court to challenge the racist policies of the University of Maryland's law school. Marshall argued that the university's policy was unconstitutional. In 1934 he got a Maryland judge to agree with his reasoning, ending the policy and forcing the school to admit Murray. Two years later Marshall shuttered his private practice to join the NAACP's national staff of lawyers. By 1940 he was the NAACP's chief attorney in charge of civil rights litigation.

In this capacity Marshall argued a number of high-profile cases, many of them before the US Supreme Court. The 1944 case *Smith v. Allwright*, for example, challenged a law in Texas that permitted the Democratic Party to limit primary elections to White voters, disenfranchising Blacks and Hispanics. Marshall helped plan a strategy that overturned the law. Several years later Marshall was victorious in *Sweatt v. Painter* and *McLaurin v. Oklahoma State Regents*, ending segregation in state-supported colleges and universities. In all, Marshall argued thirty-two cases before the Supreme Court while with the NAACP, and he won an impressive twenty-nine of them.

Brown v. Board of Education

The most famous of the Supreme Court cases Marshall worked on was a 1954 case involving segregation in public elementary, middle, and high schools. The case, *Brown v. Board of Education*, was initiated by Black families whose children were forced to attend segregated schools even though all-White schools were located much closer to their homes. (The name of the case referenced Oliver Brown of Topeka, Kansas, whose third-grade daughter, Linda, was bused a mile to an all-Black school, but the

Learning to Argue

From the time Thurgood Marshall was a child, his parents consistently encouraged their son's intellectual abilities. As he remembered it, they taught him to think for himself and to support his opinion with reasons and facts. Indeed, the family often debated current events at the dinner table. "[My father] taught me how to argue," Marshall said in 1964, "[and] challenged my logic on every point, even if we were discussing the weather." The elder Marshall also took his son to observe court cases when he could. In this environment Marshall had a chance to see lawyers making logical, well-supported arguments—and to see how judges responded to them.

Unsurprisingly, Marshall showed a keen interest in politics and government from an early age. Though Marshall's father never pushed him directly to become an attorney, Marshall saw later that he had been groomed for this job from the time he was small. "My father turned me into a lawyer without ever telling me what he wanted me to be," he said years afterward.

Quoted in Charles Moritz, ed., *Current Biography Yearbook 1989*. New York: Wilson, 1989, p. 378.

case covered families elsewhere in the country as well.) The parents in the *Brown* case argued that this segregationist policy was damaging to their children. They demanded that their children be admitted to the school of their choice.

Marshall was eager to take the case. He began by asserting that segregation was unconstitutional. As Marshall noted, the text of the Fourteenth Amendment to the US Constitution promises every citizen "the equal protection of the laws."[6] Since all-White schools almost always had better facilities and more money, Marshall argued that segregation violated this part of the amendment. He also relied on evidence from social science suggesting that segregation led to feelings of inferiority among Black children. In one famous study, Black children overwhelmingly chose to play

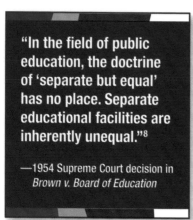

with a White doll rather than with a Black doll. The researchers concluded that Black children had low self-esteem, the result of "prejudice, discrimination, and segregation."[7]

The court released its ruling in May 1954. All nine justices accepted the NAACP's assertion that segregation was both harmful and unconstitutional. "In the field of public education," the decision read, "the doctrine of 'separate but equal' has no place. Separate educational facilities are inherently unequal."[8] Marshall and his team were elated. Legally, segregation was now a thing of the past, and schools could focus on providing the same education for everyone, regardless of race.

The court's decision seemed to be an enormous victory for Marshall and his team. In truth, the ruling was not nearly as favorable to the NAACP as it appeared. It was one thing to rule that segregation was illegal but quite another thing to actually end it. The decision was deeply unpopular in many southern states, and leaders in these states threatened to defy the ruling. The court set no timetable for desegregation, moreover, and many communities, especially in the South, found ways to continue segregating schools despite the ruling. Even today, more than sixty-five years after *Brown*, many American schools are all White, or very nearly so, while others are virtually all Black. Still, *Brown* remains a prominent and favorable ruling in the fight for integration and equality.

Judge and Solicitor General

Marshall continued to work for the NAACP for the next few years following the *Brown* decision, but in 1961 President John Kennedy offered him a new challenge by appointing him to be a judge on a federal appellate court, just one step below the US Supreme Court. Marshall knew that the position would move him away from the day-to-day struggle against racial injustice that had been his passion while at the NAACP. He also worried, at least initially, that in his absence his work would not be continued. "I had to fight it out within myself," he told a journalist, "but by then I had built up a staff—a damned good staff—an excellent board, and the [financial] backing that would let them go ahead."[9] In the end Marshall accepted Kennedy's offer.

The appointment, however, was not guaranteed. Marshall had to be confirmed by the US Senate, which included many ardent segregationists still bitter about his role in the *Brown* decision and

Thurgood Marshall, seen here in front of the US Supreme Court in 1958, argued numerous cases while with the NAACP. The most famous case was Brown v. Board of Education, *which determined that segregation in schools was unconstitutional.*

On several occasions, Thurgood Marshall became embroiled in controversy during his time on the Supreme Court. He once explained his legal philosophy, for instance, as "you do what you think is right and let the law catch up." That attitude made sense for a man who believed that laws pertaining to race were often unjust. The comment, though, alarmed conservatives who thought Marshall was ignoring the actual words of the Constitution.

In addition, Marshall gave a speech in 1987 in which he pointed out that the Constitution was an imperfect document. Marshall noted that the Constitution had originally lacked a Bill of Rights—that is, protection of basic rights such as freedom of speech and freedom of the press—and that the document had to be amended, or changed, to add these freedoms before it could be approved. Moreover, Marshall added, a civil war had been necessary to eliminate legal slavery in the country, along with a civil rights movement a century later to ensure that the laws were actually followed. Some conservatives complained that Marshall's criticisms were too dismissive of the founders of the country and failed to recognize the genius behind the Constitution.

Quoted in *Talk of the Nation*, "A Refresher Course on Thurgood Marshall," NPR, July 1, 2010. www.npr.org.

suspicious of his political liberalism. Led by Mississippi senator James Eastland, these senators drew out the process as long as they could to prevent Marshall from being approved. Indeed, Marshall was not confirmed until late 1962. As conservative senators feared, his rulings as an appellate judge did reflect a generally liberal perspective. In one case, for example, Marshall blocked the government from searching the homes of suspected criminals without following procedures designed to safeguard the suspects' rights.

Marshall could have stayed on the appellate court for the rest of his career, but in 1965 Lyndon Johnson, Kennedy's successor, convinced him to become solicitor general of the United States.

The solicitor general is a high-ranking position within the US Department of Justice, the arm of the government that enforces federal laws. In this role, Marshall argued cases for the government, many of them dealing with civil rights legislation. As solicitor general, Marshall argued nineteen cases before the Supreme Court, winning fourteen. In later life, Marshall described this post as "the best job I've ever had, bar none!"[10]

But Marshall's time as solicitor general was brief. Johnson had bigger things in mind for the new solicitor general. By moving the Appeals Court judge to the US Department of Justice, Johnson was preparing Marshall for a seat on the US Supreme Court. At the time, no Black person had ever served on the court. Johnson recognized that there would be strong opposition to the idea of a Black Supreme Court justice, especially among the most ardent segregationists in the Senate, and he wanted to ensure that Marshall's credentials were as impressive as possible. Johnson knew he could not convince everyone that nominating Marshall was, as he put it, "the right thing to do, the right time to do it, the right man and the right place."[11] But he could—and did—make certain that Marshall's background made him remarkably well qualified for the seat.

In 1967 a seat on the court became vacant, and Johnson nominated Marshall to fill it. Johnson was correct; the color of Marshall's skin was indeed a stumbling block for some southern senators. South Carolina senator Strom Thurmond subjected Marshall to a series of complex legal questions designed to make him seem ignorant. Still, in the end Marshall's nomination was approved. For the first time in history, a Black person was a Supreme Court justice.

The Supreme Court

As appellate judge, Marshall had leaned toward the left politically. That remained true while he was on the Supreme Court. He regularly voted against the death penalty, for example; his reasons included the likelihood that innocent people had suffered this fate.

"No matter how careful courts are," he wrote in a case known as *Furman v. Georgia*, "the possibility of perjured testimony, mistaken honest testimony and human error remain too real."[12] In addition to opposing capital punishment, Marshall continued his support of the rights of individuals, especially those accused of crimes.

Marshall also became known as a strong backer of the First Amendment. Part of this amendment forbids the government from punishing people for their speech or writings. Marshall worked to ensure that everyone from high school students to prisoners had the right to free speech. In addition, he was a tireless advocate for racial justice and other civil rights issues. He was a particularly strong supporter of affirmative action programs, in which Blacks and other minorities are given preference in hiring and in college admissions. "Bringing the Negro into the mainstream of American life should be a state interest of the highest order,"[13] he wrote in 1978.

Marshall served on the court until his retirement due to health issues in 1991. He died in early 1993 at age eighty-four, survived by two sons and his second wife, Cecilia (his first wife had passed away in 1955). Along with the distinction of being the first Black Supreme Court justice, Marshall is famous today for his thoughtful and often pointed decisions and arguments as a Supreme Court justice, for his victory in the *Brown* case, and for his lifelong commitment to civil rights. To Marshall himself, however, the most important part of his life was not so much the outcome as the struggle. Asked once how he wanted to be remembered, Marshall replied, "That he did what he could with what he had."[14]

CHAPTER TWO

John Lewis: Activist and US Representative

It is easy to make a list of Black civil rights activists. It is also easy to make a list of Black people who had a career in politics and related fields. Several names appear on both lists, but none are more famous—or had more influence on American laws and policies—than John Lewis. In effect, Lewis had two careers. The first career was as a civil rights leader, organizing sit-ins and other demonstrations to uphold the rights of African Americans. The second career was spent in public office, most notably serving more than thirty years in the US Congress as a representative from Georgia. In both parts of his life and work, Lewis fought tirelessly for justice and emphasized love and nonviolence. Few Americans during his life span have been more influential.

Early Years

John Lewis was born in 1940 near Troy, Alabama. His parents were farmers who earned a meager living by picking cotton, a laborious job performed from dawn to dusk under the hot southern sun. John's parents bent over again and again, making their muscles ache; thorns on the cotton plants tore at their fingers. The pay, moreover, was low, and the family struggled to get by. At times

John was pressed into service picking cotton, too, but even as a child he was aware of the inadequate pay and the unfairness of their situation. "Working for nothing, that's what I would tell my mother we were doing,"[15] he remembered years later.

Poverty was not the only issue the Lewis family faced. Alabama was one of the most heavily segregated states in the country, and John accordingly grew up in a society in which Blacks and Whites rarely mixed. He attended segregated schools, riding in rickety school buses to tumble-down school buildings while White children had newer buses and well-appointed schools. He grew up with a strong revulsion to segregation and all that it meant. "From my earliest memories," he wrote, "I could feel in my bones that segregation was wrong, and I felt I had an obligation to change it."[16]

> "From my earliest memories I could feel in my bones that segregation was wrong, and I felt I had an obligation to change it."[16]
>
> —John Lewis

John's boyhood experiences helped him see how the world might be a different place. One reason was an abiding hunger for education. Despite the substandard schools he attended, John loved learning and read enthusiastically. At age eleven, he also benefited from a trip to visit relatives in Buffalo, New York. Unlike Alabama, Buffalo was not segregated, and John became aware that there were places where Blacks and Whites could live in relative harmony. "It was another world," he remembered. He was particularly impressed that White families lived next door to his relatives—as he put it, "on *both* sides."[17]

John's religious faith, too, led him to believe that there was a better way. The Christian message of Jesus's sacrifice on behalf of all humankind appealed to John. From early on he saw himself in the role of a minister; as a boy he even began preaching to his family's flock of chickens. As a teenager, John's passion for justice, education, and religion came together when he heard Martin Luther King Jr. speak on the radio. King was a pastor in addition

In 1963 civil rights leaders, including John Lewis, planned a protest in Washington, DC. Known as the March on Washington, it is famous today as the site of Martin Luther King's "I Have a Dream" speech. Lewis was one of the speakers at the demonstration. Part of his speech implored Black people and sympathetic Whites across the country to support the movement. "I appeal to all of you to get into this great revolution that is sweeping the nation," he said.

> Get in and stay in the streets of every city, every village and hamlet of this nation until true freedom comes, until the revolution of 1776 is complete. We must get in this revolution and complete the revolution. For in the Delta in Mississippi, in southwest Georgia, in the Black Belt of Alabama, in Harlem, in Chicago, Detroit, Philadelphia, and all over this nation, the black masses are on the march for jobs and freedom.

Lewis had wanted to go further. President John Kennedy had supported a weak civil rights bill, and in his speech Lewis wanted to press Kennedy to strengthen the bill. However, he was overruled by other leaders who feared that the president might be offended.

Quoted in Voices of Democracy, "John Lewis: Speech at the March on Washington (28 August 1963)." https://voicesofdemocracy.umd.edu.

to being a civil rights leader, and his words resounded with John. "I felt he was talking directly to me," he remembered. "From that moment on, I decided I wanted to be just like him."[18] He enrolled in an all-Black college in Nashville, Tennessee, where he studied for the ministry.

Integration and Sit-Ins

In 1958, encouraged by the story of Black students who integrated Little Rock High School in Arkansas, Lewis decided that he was called to integrate the all-white Troy State College in his hometown. He sought advice from none other than King, who met with Lewis—or, as King referred to him, "the boy from Troy."[19] King was supportive but warned Lewis that he and his family would likely suffer consequences for his stand. Lewis's parents, King explained, might lose their jobs; even violence was a possibility. In the end Lewis's parents asked him not to try to integrate the college. Lewis reluctantly agreed and returned to his studies in Tennessee.

But Lewis continued his activism for civil rights. As a student he led sit-ins at segregated lunch counters in downtown Nashville, demonstrated for Black voting rights, and organized measures to

John Lewis stands in front of the Capitol Building in 1998. Lewis set his sights well beyond issues of special relevance to Black people, addressing concerns such as gun safety legislation and gay rights.

desegregate the city's department stores. In the process, Lewis was arrested several times, usually on charges of disturbing the peace during the sit-ins. "I grew up sitting down on those lunch counter stools and going to jail,"[20] Lewis said once. The protesters adhered to King's doctrine of nonviolence, even when White thugs punched them, sprayed them with detergent, or banged their heads against the counters. "Don't strike back or curse back if abused,"[21] Lewis instructed those taking part in the sit-ins, and they did not.

The protests were successful. The publicity generated by the sit-ins put these segregationist policies in a very bad light, and in May 1960 segregation at the city's lunch counters came to an end. Lewis acknowledged that the protesters had run significant risks but congratulated them for getting into what he called "good trouble, necessary trouble"[22] — a phrase that would describe and define Lewis's career.

> "I grew up sitting down on those lunch counter stools and going to jail."[20]
>
> —John Lewis

Freedom Rides and the Edmund Pettus Bridge

In 1960 Lewis also became a member of a student group called the Student Nonviolent Coordinating Committee, or SNCC. The following year he helped lead efforts to desegregate intercity buses and bus waiting rooms throughout the South. The US Supreme Court had ruled the previous year that this type of segregation was illegal, but southern states largely ignored the court's decision. In response, Lewis helped organize what became known as Freedom Rides. He and other young men and women, some Black and others White, took buses into the South to challenge the segregation in bus terminals.

The Freedom Riders were repeatedly harassed and sometimes assaulted along the way. Lewis was badly beaten at a South Carolina bus station while police officers looked on, for example. Later, in Alabama, he was knocked unconscious by a

John Lewis was typically optimistic, but in the wake of the beating he suffered on the Edmund Pettus Bridge in Selma, he began to grow discouraged. The opposition to the civil rights movement seemed more entrenched than he had suspected, and he began to see the limitations of nonviolence in what seemed to be an increasingly violent world. He questioned why he—or anyone else—would continue to risk their lives under these circumstances. "We're only flesh," he said. "I could understand people not wanting to get beaten anymore."

At the same time, Lewis continued to maintain that violence was not the answer. In this he found himself increasingly at odds with more militant activists within the movement, some of whom were rejecting the entire concept of nonviolence. In 1966 a more radical activist, Stokely Carmichael, defeated Lewis in an election for SNCC chair. Soon Lewis left the organization altogether. "It was the bitterness all around that turned me," he told an interviewer. "A program based on violence . . . might deliver some quick solutions, but in the long run it debases you."

Quoted in Charles Moritz, ed., *Current Biography Yearbook 1980*. New York: Wilson, 1980, p. 224.

man wielding a club. Angry Whites once burned a bus on which Freedom Riders were traveling. Still, Lewis continued to believe that nonviolence was the answer. And indeed, the efforts of the Freedom Riders paid off. Later in 1961 the Interstate Commerce Commission, which made rules regarding interstate bus travel, ordered all bus stations to be integrated.

Lewis became the national chair of SNCC in 1963. Two years later he was in the headlines again when he and King organized a march to protest restrictive voting rights in Alabama. As the marchers crossed the Edmund Pettus Bridge leading out of the town of Selma, they were attacked by law enforcement personnel. Lewis's skull was fractured. But once again his actions helped bring about change. Many people outside the South were appalled to see the violence unleashed on the peaceful protesters, and later that year President Lyndon Johnson signed the Voting Rights Act, a comprehensive bill that protected the right to vote even in southern states.

By 1966 Lewis's days in the trenches of the civil rights movement were largely over. His commitment to racial equality and social justice, however, was not. Over the next few years, Lewis held a variety of jobs, mostly focused on child welfare, voting rights, or the rural poor. He also married another activist, Lillian Miles. The couple had one son, John-Miles.

As time went on, though, Lewis began to consider a more expressly political career. In 1977 he ran for an open seat in the US House of Representatives from his new home in Atlanta, Georgia. Lewis lost to a White man, a fellow Democrat named Wyche Fowler, but took a job working on social programs in the administration of Democratic president Jimmy Carter. However. Lewis found his initiatives thwarted by bureaucracy and budgetary issues and resigned in 1980. The following year he ran for, and won, a seat on the Atlanta City Council. When Fowler decided to run for the US Senate in 1986, Lewis opted for another run for the House. This time he unexpectedly defeated fellow civil rights leader Julian Bond in what one journalist called a "bitterly divisive"[23] campaign. He took office in 1987.

Representative Lewis

In the eyes of most observers, Lewis proved more than capable as a political leader. The voters of his district certainly thought so, as they regularly reelected him by substantial margins. In the end he served nearly seventeen terms in Congress, from 1987 until his death in 2020. Indeed, Lewis became known within the Democratic Party as the "conscience of the Congress"[24] for his principled stands. These stands included continued vigilance in protecting civil rights for African Americans. He was an early and enthusiastic supporter of the Black Lives Matter movement, for example, which he said reminded him of the civil rights movement of the 1960s in its goals and methods. Lewis also worked hard in Congress to safeguard voting rights for Black people and other minorities.

Lewis set his sights well beyond issues of special relevance to Black people, though. For example, he was deeply distrustful of war. He opposed the Gulf War in 1991 and the war against Iraq in 2003. Lewis also fought hard for gun safety legislation. At one point he staged a sit-in on the floor of the House of Representatives demanding that a gun control bill come up for a vote. And Lewis was a strong supporter of gay rights. "I've heard the reasons for opposing civil marriage for same-sex couples," he wrote in 2003, long before most liberal politicians supported marriage equality. "Cut through the distractions, and they stink of the same fear, hatred, and intolerance I have known in racism and in bigotry."[25]

As a political liberal, Lewis often criticized Republicans and conservatives. He had a particular distaste for Republican president George W. Bush; Lewis boycotted Bush's first inauguration, arguing that the president's victory was not legitimate. Later, he likened President Donald Trump to former Alabama governor and ardent segregationist George Wallace. "I think demagogues are pretty dangerous," Lewis said of Trump. "We shouldn't divide people, we shouldn't separate people."[26] But Lewis also took on Democratic presidents when he opposed their positions. He sharply criticized Bill Clinton, for example, when Clinton pushed for a welfare reform bill that Lewis believed was deeply flawed.

Within the Democratic Party, Lewis's influence was especially strong. In 2008 he switched his support during the primaries from Hillary Clinton to Barack Obama, a move that encouraged other Black leaders to do the same. "People are prepared and ready to

> "I've heard the reasons for opposing civil marriage for same-sex couples. Cut through the distractions, and they stink of the same fear, hatred, and intolerance I have known in racism and in bigotry."[25]
>
> —John Lewis

make that great leap"[27] of supporting an African American candidate, Lewis said at the time. Lewis had an impact on the Democratic presidential race in 2020, too. Democratic candidate Joe Biden had promised to choose a woman as his running mate, and Lewis recommended that the woman be non-White. Biden had many reasons for choosing Kamala Harris as his vice presidential candidate, but Lewis's preference that Biden choose a non-White woman likely played a role.

Death and Legacy

Lewis was diagnosed with pancreatic cancer in late 2019. "I have been in some kind of fight—for freedom, equality, basic human rights—for nearly my entire life," he said. "I have never faced a fight quite like the one I have now."[28] He remained in office and continued to work on the issues that mattered to him. In July 2020, however, Lewis died. His funeral casket was ceremonially driven across the Edmund Pettus Bridge. Then his body lay in state, first in Alabama, then in the Capitol in Washington, DC, and finally in his adopted home city of Atlanta. He had gone from the child of poor farmers to being one of the best-known leaders of the twentieth and twenty-first centuries, and people around the country mourned his loss.

To the end, even in what often appeared to be a dangerously divided nation, Lewis maintained his optimism. "I think there's something brewing in America that's going to bring people closer and closer together," he wrote shortly before his death. "We need a leadership of love now, a strong leadership to lift us, to transport us, to remind us that God's truth is marching on. We can do it. We must do it. We have to go forward as one people, one family, one house. I believe in it. I believe we can do it. . . . It's all going to work out."[29] That steadfast assurance that things could and would be better was perhaps the defining characteristic of John Lewis's life and work.

CHAPTER THREE

Barack Obama: US President

Barack Obama's career has included stints as a community organizer, law professor, and civil rights attorney, but he is best known for his work in electoral politics. In 2008, after just over a decade as a political office-holder, Obama won the Democratic Party's presidential nomination, making him the first Black person to be a presidential candidate from a major party. Then, that November, he won the general election to become the first African American president. Obama's election delighted and inspired millions, not least because of the major barrier Obama had broken. As one journalist put it, "No child—black or white—will ever grow up again in an America thinking that a black man will never be elected president."[30]

Childhood to Law School

Barack Obama's family background is quite unlike that of any other American president. His mother, Ann Dunham, was a White American anthropologist; his father, Barack Obama Sr., was a Black economist from Kenya. Barack's parents met and married when they were both students at the University of Hawaii, and their son, officially named Barack Hussein Obama II, was born in Hawaii in 1961. The marriage did not last long, however, and Barack's father returned to Kenya. Ann remarried in 1965 to Lolo

Soetoro, a geographer from Indonesia. When Barack was six, he moved with his mother and stepfather to Indonesia, where he attended Indonesian-language schools. His mother supplemented his Indonesian education with English lessons, including recordings of speeches by Martin Luther King Jr.

At age ten, Barack returned to Hawaii to live with his grandparents so he could attend an American school. He remained in Hawaii through his high school graduation in 1979. Hawaii was and is one of the most racially and ethnically diverse of the American states, and along with his years in Indonesia, he credits his experience in Hawaii with helping him develop a multicultural worldview. At the same time, Barack's half-African ancestry often made him feel uncomfortable while he was growing up. "A redheaded girl asked to touch my hair," he recalled of his first day at school in Hawaii, "and seemed hurt when I refused. A ruddy-faced boy asked me if my father ate people."[31] As a teenager, Barack experimented with drugs, partly in an attempt to alleviate the separateness he felt. Still, he was a good student who was generally well liked by his classmates.

After high school, Obama went to Occidental College in California and then to Columbia University in New York. He studied political science with an emphasis on international relations, an interest sparked in part by his family's diverse background. "When we get together for Christmas or Thanksgiving, it's like a little mini-United Nations," he told talk show host Oprah Winfrey in 2006. "I've got relatives who look like [Black comedian] Bernie Mac, and relatives who look like [White politician] Margaret Thatcher."[32] In 1985 Obama moved to the South Side of Chicago, where he spent three years as a community organizer before enrolling at Harvard Law School in 1988.

> "When we get together for Christmas or Thanksgiving, it's like a little mini-United Nations. I've got relatives who look like [Black comedian] Bernie Mac, and relatives who look like [White politician] Margaret Thatcher."[32]
>
> —Barack Obama

In 2000 Barack Obama decided to try for higher office by challenging US representative Bobby Rush in the Democratic primary for a House seat. Rush, an African American, was a former radical in the civil rights movement. He was also a veteran lawmaker with strong support in his heavily Black district based in the South Side of Chicago. Still, Obama believed voters in the district might be ready for a fresh face and new ideas.

He was wrong. Rush won the primary by a margin of about two to one. Many Black voters were suspicious of Obama's roots outside the district. They also appreciated Rush's sacrifices during the civil rights movement and thought that Obama lacked credibility as a leader. "It was an ugly race," says author David Remnick. "Obama was deeply hurt by it. A community that he thought he was part of, that he had aspired to, had rejected him and rejected him soundly." Obama thought briefly about quitting electoral politics altogether, but eventually thought better of it. It was a wise decision: just four years later he won his seat in the US Senate.

Quoted in *Morning Edition*, "Remnick: In Obama's Only Loss, a Political Lesson." NPR, April 6, 2010. www.npr.org.

Obama had been a good student in the past, but his work at Harvard was outstanding. He was chosen to be editor (and later, president) of the school's legal journal, the *Harvard Law Review*. He graduated in 1991 near the top of his class and returned to Chicago to teach at the University of Chicago Law School. He also wrote a book, *Dreams from My Father*, and worked as an attorney on issues related to civil rights, voter registration, and economic development. In addition, he married Michelle Robinson in 1992; the couple has two children, Malia and Sasha. Obama frequently refers to his wife and children as inspirations. "In the end, girls," he wrote in a letter to his daughters published in *Parade* magazine, "that's why I ran for President: because of what I want for you and for every child in this nation."[33]

The Illinois State Senate

In 1996 Obama entered electoral politics by running for and winning a seat in the Illinois Senate. As a state senator Obama worked on issues such as expanding health care for children, providing funds for community organizations in Chicago's poorer neighborhoods, and equal pay for women. He won reelection twice, each time with no significant opposition. He aspired to higher office, however, and in 2004 he saw his chance. Incumbent US senator Peter Fitzgerald decided not to run for reelection that year, and Obama was one of many who entered the race to succeed him. Obama worked hard to reach out to voters and saw his efforts pay off in the Democratic primary when he won more than twice as many votes as any other candidate.

The size of Obama's primary victory was unexpected, and political observers began to wonder where this young African American's career might eventually take him. The media flocked to Illinois to cover Obama's campaign and introduce him to the rest of the country. "Some of us realized he could be president," remembered political consultant Kevin Lampe, whose enthusiasm was tempered only by Obama's race, "but you know, they're never going to elect an African-American president."[34] Still, even if becoming president seemed impossible, there was no question that Obama was a remarkable politician. As John Kerry, the Democratic presidential candidate in 2004, put it, "[Obama] should be one of the faces of our party now, not years from now."[35]

Kerry meant what he said. Though Obama was still just a state senator, Kerry offered him the chance to give the keynote speech at the Democratic National Convention that July. Lampe and others worried that Obama might flub the opportunity; Obama had never been regarded as a particularly strong speaker. But their concerns were ungrounded. Obama gave a speech that turned him into a sensation. In part, his delivery was masterful, even mesmerizing. "It was like he had 10,000 sets of eyes," remembers political consultant Valerie Jarrett, "like he was looking into everyone's eyes and talking one-on-one with everyone in the room."[36]

The message of the speech resonated with the audience too. Obama described his gratitude toward his family—"I stand here today," he said, "grateful for the diversity of my heritage, aware that my parents' dreams live on in my two precious daughters"—before turning his attention to questions of poverty, education, and war. He focused also on the need to work together and stressed the commonalities among Americans. "There is not a liberal America and a conservative America," he argued; "there is the United States of America. . . . We worship an awesome God in the Blue States, and we don't like federal agents poking around in our libraries in the Red States."[37] The speech made Obama famous across America and sparked discussion that, despite his race, he might actually become president someday.

> "There is not a liberal America and a conservative America; there is the United States of America. . . . We worship an awesome God in the Blue States, and we don't like federal agents poking around in our libraries in the Red States."[37]
>
> —Barack Obama

A Presidential Run

That fall, Obama defeated Republican Alan Keyes in the Senate race with more than two-thirds of the vote. He took his seat in early 2005, making him the only African American in the Senate at the time (several Black people had served in the Senate previously, including one from Illinois). Aware that he knew little about international relations, Obama spent much of his first two years in office working on foreign policy issues. If he were to run for president, Obama reasoned, he wanted to be as knowledgeable about the issues as possible.

As the 2008 presidential election approached, Obama examined his options. Young and inexperienced, he was still only about halfway through his first term as senator. "Obviously," said adviser David Axelrod, "if people decided that what they ultimately wanted was years of Washington experience, he would not be the nominee."[38] But Obama thought people were ready for a fresh face with new ideas. He also believed that 2008 might be his best chance to run for many years; if he wanted to be president, this was the time. In early 2007 Obama declared his intention to run for the Democratic presidential nomination.

Despite Obama's star power, many observers gave him little chance of winning the nomination. Several politicians with much more experience were running. One popular candidate was Hillary Clinton, a senator from New York and former First Lady, who had strong support from many people she had worked with over the years—including Black leaders such as representatives John Lewis and Elijah Cummings. Nonetheless, Obama developed a powerful political organization and won an unexpected victory

Barack Obama speaks during his 2008 presidential campaign. Obama went on to defeat Republican senator John McCain in the election and became the first African American president.

CHANGE
WE NEED
WWW.BARACKOBAMA.COM

in the Iowa caucus, the first event of the primary season. When Obama won decisively in South Carolina a few weeks later, Lewis and others began switching their support to him.

The race was tight, but in the end Obama narrowly won the nomination. In his acceptance speech at the Democratic convention, he outlined the actions he intended to take if elected and drew sharp distinctions between himself and the Republican nominee, Arizona senator John McCain. He also spoke of the need for cooperation between the political parties and among ordinary Americans. "What . . . has been lost," he told the convention delegates, "is our sense of common purpose—our sense of higher purpose. And that's what we have to restore."[39] That fall he defeated McCain, winning 365 of 538 electoral votes to become the nation's first African American president. Four years later, Obama defeated another Republican, former Massachusetts governor Mitt Romney, to earn a second term in office.

Obama's Presidency

As president, Obama took a generally liberal stance on the issues. He is best known for the Affordable Care Act, which helped people lacking health insurance purchase the coverage they needed; estimates suggest that the act extended insurance to at least 20 million people who had previously gone without. Obama was also a strong advocate for gun control. "We're going to have to come together and take meaningful action to prevent more tragedies like this,"[40] he said after a mass shooting in Newtown, Connecticut. While he came into office opposed to marriage equality, his views slowly changed; by mid-2012 he was on record as supporting the right of gays and lesbians to marry. Obama also focused on protecting abortion rights, stricter regulation of banks, and lessening the impact of climate change.

Not all of Obama's actions were applauded by his party's most liberal voters, however. Some Democrats believed, for example, that his regulation of the banks did not go nearly far enough. In addition, many liberals argued that the Affordable Care Act should

First Inaugural Address

Barack Obama's first inauguration took place on January 20, 2009. His speech that day focused on the challenges that lay ahead, as well as on the values that he believed had made the United States a great country. As he put it during the address:

> Our challenges may be new. The instruments with which we meet them may be new. But those values upon which our success depends—honesty and hard work, courage and fair play, tolerance and curiosity, loyalty and patriotism—these things are old. These things are true. They have been the quiet force of progress throughout our history. What is demanded then is a return to these truths. What is required of us now is a new era of responsibility—a recognition, on the part of every American, that we have duties to ourselves, our nation, and the world, duties that we do not grudgingly accept but rather seize gladly, firm in the knowledge that there is nothing so satisfying to the spirit, so defining of our character, than giving our all to a difficult task.

Quoted in NPR, "Transcript: Barack Obama's Inaugural Address," January 20, 2009. www.npr.org.

have covered everyone, not just the uninsured. But the strongest opposition to Obama and his policies came from the Republican Party. Very few Republicans in Congress voted for any of Obama's proposals, and Senate Majority Leader Mitch McConnell said in a 2010 interview that "the single most important thing we want to achieve is for President Obama to be a one-term president."[41] Obama made many efforts to gain Republican support for his initiatives, but almost without exception they were rebuffed. Still, McConnell's desire was not realized; Obama was reelected in 2012.

Obama could point to several other important achievements while in office. When he was first elected, for example, the United States had just experienced a sudden economic downturn.

Obama's actions helped prop up companies and workers to minimize the impact of the event; before long the economy was growing again, and it continued to expand throughout Obama's two terms as president. In addition, Osama bin Laden, the mastermind behind the attacks of September 11, 2001, had evaded capture ever since the tragedy, but he was located and killed during Obama's time in office. And Obama won the Nobel Peace Prize in 2009 for his work on limiting nuclear weapons and developing better relationships with the Muslim world.

Staying Involved

Obama left the White House in 2017, after his two terms in office were over. He remained in Washington and spoke out occasionally on important issues of the day, taking positions that were in sharp opposition to his successor as president, Donald Trump. For instance, he made a statement opposing the 2017 US withdrawal from the Paris Agreement, an international treaty regarding climate change. He also criticized the Trump administration's immigration policies and its response to the COVID-19 crisis that hit America and the rest of the world in 2020. More generally, as Obama put it, the Trump administration had resulted in "our worst impulses unleashed, our proud reputation around the world badly diminished, and our democratic institutions threatened like never before."[42] In the presidential election of 2020, Obama strongly supported Joe Biden, his vice president for both of his presidential terms, and worked hard to ensure Biden's election.

No one knows what the future holds for Obama—perhaps not even Obama himself. Many former presidents retreat to a relatively low-profile and nonpartisan life, but Obama seems likely to continue his involvement in the political and governmental sphere for some time to come. He and Michelle have established the Obama Foundation, whose mission is to "inspire, empower, and connect people to change their world,"[43] and his name has been mentioned as a possible candidate for Supreme Court justice if a vacancy arises when a Democratic president is in power. Whatever happens, his place in history is assured.

CHAPTER FOUR

Stacey Abrams: Voting Rights Activist

Just as Barack Obama went from being virtually unknown to becoming a member of the US Senate, and then the president, Stacey Abrams appeared to come out of nowhere when she ran for governor of Georgia in 2018. As a Black female candidate for the governorship of a southern state, Abrams captured the imagination of many Americans—and the media as well. "In a Democratic Party divided and desperate for new faces," wrote journalist Molly Ball, "Abrams is already becoming a national star."[44] And though Abrams narrowly lost the election, she stayed in the public eye by working tirelessly for voting rights in the South and elsewhere. Following her meteoric rise, Abrams remains a powerful force in both politics and the civil rights movement.

Early Life

Stacey Abrams was born in 1973 in Wisconsin, where her mother was working on a graduate degree in library science. Soon after her birth, Stacey's family returned to their roots in Gulfport, Mississippi. Her mother got a low-paying job as a college librarian; her father, despite having a college degree, worked as a laborer in a shipyard. Even in the 1970s, racism was an issue in the Deep South. "They went away for education," says Abrams of her parents, "but when they got back to Mississippi, they were still black."[45] At times the family could not pay their bills, resulting in water or electrical services being shut off until they could find the money they needed.

When Stacey was in high school, her family moved again—this time to Atlanta, Georgia, where her parents were studying to become ministers. Stacey was valedictorian of her high school—the first African American to earn that distinction—and was chosen to attend a program in Ithaca, New York, for high-achieving students. Once in Ithaca, though, she felt outclassed. As she put it, her fellow students "referenced books I'd never read and scholars I hadn't heard of." She begged her parents to take her home, but they refused—and, she reflected afterward, they were right. "I had always been smart," she recalled, "but I needed to test myself against those who were smarter, more talented, and more accomplished."[46]

> "I had always been smart, but I needed to test myself against those who were smarter, more talented, and more accomplished."[46]
>
> —Stacey Abrams

Abrams's interest in politics goes back to her high school years, too. At age seventeen she took a job as a typist for a congressional campaign. "I edited [the candidate's] speech, which I was given to type," she remembers, "and he actually promoted me to becoming a speechwriter!" In addition to boosting her confidence and giving her valuable experience, the incident taught her that doing things is far preferable to not doing things. "I was with a group of young people who were all offered the opportunity to volunteer with his campaign," she told an interviewer, "and I was the only one who took it. . . . You don't know what you're going to be allowed to do, but you'll be allowed to do absolutely nothing if you aren't there."[47]

College and Civil Rights

Abrams continued her education at Spelman College, a historically Black women's college in Atlanta. Like the summer program

Those Who Inspired Abrams

Stacey Abrams cites quite a few civil rights leaders over the years, many of them Black women, as inspirations. Some of these influences go back well over a century. One inspiration, for example, was Harriet Tubman, an enslaved person in Maryland who helped lead dozens, perhaps hundreds, of people out of slavery and into freedom. Another was abolitionist and women's rights advocate Sojourner Truth. Among more recent figures, Abrams particularly admires Fannie Lou Hamer, a combative civil rights activist of the 1960s from whom, as author Martha S. Jones puts it, Abrams "learned to stand her ground, use the podium and the press, and play the long game."

Abrams also has been inspired by people closer to home, notably her parents and grandparents. She was impressed by her parents' determination to make the best possible life for themselves and their children and for their roles in the civil rights movement. Her grandparents were not directly involved in the movement, fearing that they might lose their jobs or even their lives, but they did bail her father out of jail when he was arrested for trying to register Black people to vote in Mississippi. All were inspirations to Abrams.

Martha S. Jones, *Vanguard*. New York: Basic, 2020, p. 274.

in New York, Spelman helped open Abrams's eyes to the wider world. "I found myself seeing how much blacks could achieve," she writes. "My new classmates were the daughters of politicians and famous lawyers and corporate leaders. . . . I was now in a context that included people of color, women no less, who had confidence that they could succeed."[48] Even so, Abrams still believed that her options were limited by her race and gender. "My highest ambition when I was in college thinking about politics was to become mayor of Atlanta," she remembers, "because that was the highest [political] job I'd ever seen a Black woman have."[49]

Civil rights issues also occupied some of Abrams's time as a college student. In 1992 a Black man named Rodney King was savagely beaten by police officers in California. Four of the officers were charged with using excessive force, but none were convicted. Following the verdict, riots broke out in many cities around the country, including Atlanta. Abrams was appalled by the police response to the rioting, which involved cordoning off areas and spraying protesters with tear gas—actions that she felt were heavy handed, racist, and counterproductive.

As she watched the news, moreover, Abrams heard commentators dismissing Atlanta's Blacks as angry vandals whose goal in life was simply to destroy property and disturb the peace. Abrams believed the situation was much more complicated than that. She called one of the news stations to complain about its coverage, but the person who took the call hung up on her. Abrams then organized other Spelman students to deluge all the Atlanta stations with complaints, telling them to use her name if they were not comfortable using their own.

Stacey Abrams campaigns during the race for governor of Georgia in 2018. The election shed light on the issue of voter suppression, a problem that Abrams continues to fight against.

Though many of the students' calls did get through, they had no effect on the coverage. Still, the calls did get Abrams an invitation to appear on a televised community town hall to discuss the rioting. The mayor, a Black man named Maynard Jackson, was also present. Abrams listened to Jackson's angry words about the rioters and eventually confronted him, asking what he had done for the impoverished Black youth of Atlanta, who had to deal with drugs and gangs and often felt alienated from the rest of the city. Jackson responded by telling her how far the city had come—and a few months later, struck by her passion and intelligence, gave her a part-time job working in the city's Office of Youth Services.

The Georgia House of Representatives

Following her time at Spelman, Abrams left Atlanta to earn a graduate degree in public policy at the University of Texas. In 1999 she added a law degree from Yale University to her résumé. Returning to Atlanta, Abrams worked for several years as an attorney in a large law firm, then served as Atlanta's deputy city attorney. In 2006 she decided to run for a seat in the Georgia House of Representatives. "I understood that government has a tremendous capacity to help people unlock their own potential," Abrams writes, explaining why she chose to enter the race, "and I wanted a job where I could foster change for families like mine."[50] She won the Democratic primary in a heavily Democratic district, defeating two better-known opponents, and then won the general election easily.

"I understood that government has a tremendous capacity to help people unlock their own potential, and I wanted a job where I could foster change for families like mine."[50]

—Stacey Abrams

The Republican Party had a majority in the state House throughout Abrams's time in office, and in 2010 Abrams's Democratic colleagues voted her to the post of House minority leader—the highest-ranking Democrat in the House. Being in leadership was a great honor for Abrams, but it also presented a problem. Minority leaders are typically loud and combative; certainly Abrams's predecessor in the post, fellow Democrat DuBose Porter, had acted that way. As a woman of color, though, Abrams worried that following Porter's example would be a bad idea. It was one thing for a White man like Porter to yell at Republicans, but a Black woman who did the same, Abrams reasoned, would be perceived as rude and angry.

Abrams accordingly adopted a much more subdued approach to leadership. As she writes, "I leaned more intentionally on wordsmithing and incisiveness than volume." Many of her fellow Democrats disapproved of this decision. "I found myself immediately criticized by my colleagues for not being more voluble and visibly indignant,"[51] she notes. However, Abrams remained confident that her tactics were correct. Indeed, she was willing to work with the Republicans—to a point. In one instance she worked with the state's governor, Republican Nathan Deal, to pass criminal justice reforms. In another, however, she blocked a Republican bill that would have increased taxes on the great majority of Georgia residents.

A Gubernatorial Race

Abrams remained in the state legislature until 2017, when she resigned her seat to run for governor. She proved to be an able campaigner who earned a reputation as a charismatic speaker. "People tend to remember the first time they heard Stacey Abrams speak,"[52] writes a journalist who covered the campaign. Abrams won the Democratic primary easily and then faced Secretary of State Brian Kemp in the general election. Despite the publicity Abrams was receiving worldwide for her run, she was facing an uphill battle. No African American woman had ever been elected governor of any state—part of the reason the media found her so interesting—and the Republicans held every statewide office in Georgia.

There was another issue as well. One of the duties of Georgia's secretary of state is to oversee the voter rolls. In 2017, after Kemp announced that he would be running for governor, he removed seven hundred thousand people from the rolls, including half a million in a single evening. "This purge, according to election-law experts," wrote Alan Judd, a reporter for an Atlanta newspaper the next day, "may represent the largest mass disenfranchisement in U.S. history."[53] Kemp argued that he was justified in removing the voters, as some had moved and others had not voted in several elections, but Abrams and her allies charged that Kemp was removing people who should not have been removed as well. Kemp, Abrams said, was misusing his authority in an effort to reduce turnout, especially among minority groups.

> "This purge, according to election-law experts, may represent the largest mass disenfranchisement in U.S. history."[53]
>
> —Alan Judd, journalist

Kemp's plans to restrict voting continued into 2018 as well. Shortly before the election, his office refused to process more than fifty thousand applications from prospective new voters. More than three-quarters of these applicants were racial minorities, the great majority of them Black. Kemp argued that these applications violated Georgia's "exact match" law, which held that names on voter application forms must precisely match names in other government records, such as Social Security cards and drivers' licenses. Again, though, Abrams sharply criticized Kemp's actions, calling him "a remarkable architect of voter suppression."[54]

Kemp won the election by less than fifty thousand votes, a victory that Abrams and her allies attributed primarily to Kemp's actions in canceling registrations and placing applications on hold. She considered going to court to try to have the election results overturned, but she eventually decided against it. Still, she remained convinced that the election had been stolen from her. Abrams also filed suit in federal court charging Kemp and Georgia's board of elections with illegal suppression of voters; as of late 2021 a ruling had not yet been made.

Stacey Abrams is best known as a political activist, but there are other sides to her as well. As a young woman she set herself the goal of becoming a millionaire by the time she was thirty, and while that goal proved elusive, she has started several corporations. In fact, in news stories she has been called a "serial entrepreneur" based on the number and variety of companies she has founded, either alone or with business partner Lara O'Connor Hodgson. Among others, these companies include Insomnia Consulting, which focuses on securing funding for infrastructure projects; Nourish Inc., which manufactured beverages for babies; and financial services firm NOWAccount Network Corporation.

Abrams is also a fiction writer who has published eight romantic suspense novels using the pen name Selena Montgomery. In recent years she has stopped publishing fiction to focus instead on her political career, but she hopes to get back into writing in the future. She has ideas for at least one more Montgomery novel and also hopes to complete the manuscript of a legal thriller in addition to writing books for children and young adults.

PR Newswire, "Former Georgia House of Representatives Minority Leader Stacey Abrams Added to TriNet PeopleForce Roster of Esteemed Speakers," August 17, 2021. www.prnewswire.com.

The 2020 Election

Although Abrams had officially lost the race, her star continued to rise. The Democratic Party chose her to give the party's response to Donald Trump's State of the Union speech in January 2019, an honor often given to up-and-coming politicians. Democratic Senate leader Chuck Schumer also pressured Abrams to run for one of the two US Senate seats that would be contested in Georgia in 2020. But Abrams turned him down. "The fights to be waged require a deep commitment to the job," she said, "and I do not see the U.S. Senate as the best role for me in this battle for our nation's future."[55]

That decision did not mean, however, that Abrams would drop out of politics altogether. Instead, she chose to focus her work on advocating for unbiased elections and voting rights. She founded an organization called Fair Fight Action, which works to register new voters and to protect existing voters from being removed from the rolls. "We are still mired in a past of voter suppression," she told a group of supporters in 2019. "And voter intimidation. And mistakes made. But we are going to correct those mistakes. . . . I'm going to use my energies and my very, very loud voice to raise the money we need."[56]

Abrams's work paid off. In November 2020, much to the surprise of political pundits, Georgia went narrowly for Democratic candidate Joe Biden over incumbent Donald Trump. It was the first time since 1992 that Georgia's electoral votes had gone to a Democratic candidate, and while Biden of course received much of the credit for winning the state, Abrams received plenty of accolades as well. "He could not have done it without Stacey Abrams,"[57] a team of journalists wrote following the result. In addition, both Senate races in Georgia were won by the Democratic candidate, giving the party a majority in each house of Congress. Again, Abrams garnered well-deserved praise for her role in getting the senators elected.

In late 2021, Abrams announced her next step: a rematch against Kemp for Georgia's governorship in 2022. She also intends to continue her work securing voters' rights and working for fair elections. Abrams has spoken about possibly running for president in 2028 and has gone so far as to say that she expects to be elected to the office sometime in the next twenty years. "That's my plan,"[58] she told a reporter. Whatever direction Abrams chooses to take in the coming decades, she has already had an enormous effect on politics—and will undoubtedly continue to do the same in the future.

CHAPTER FIVE

Kamala Harris: US Vice President

The first woman, first African American, and first Asian American to serve as vice president of the United States, Kamala Harris has had a long and impressive career in law and government. While John Lewis, Martin Luther King Jr., and many other important Black leaders focused on changing the system from the outside, Harris typically focused on challenging injustice from inside the system—as prosecutor, attorney general, US senator, and vice president. As she writes, "There was an important role on the inside, sitting at the table where decisions were being made. When activists came marching and banging on the doors, I wanted to be on the other side to let them in."[59] Few African American leaders have matched Harris's effectiveness at working within the system.

Childhood and Education

Kamala Harris was born in Oakland, California, in 1964. Like Barack Obama, she was the product of an interracial marriage at a time when such relationships were much less common than they are today. Just as Obama's father was born and raised outside the United States, so too was Harris's; her father, an economist named Donald J. Harris, was a Black man originally from Jamaica. Unlike Obama, though, Harris had two parents who were not American by birth. Her mother, Shyamala Gopalan, was a cancer researcher who grew up in India. Harris's parents met in California while taking part in the civil rights movement and married soon afterward. After Kamala was born, they often brought her to protest rallies with them. "It's because of them and the folks who also took to the streets to fight for justice that I am where I am,"[60] Harris once wrote.

The marriage, however, did not last. The couple separated in the late 1960s, soon after Kamala's sister, Maya, was born. Not long afterward they divorced. "They didn't fight about money," Harris notes wryly. "The only thing they fought about was who got the books." Though the Harris sisters continued to see their father, they lived primarily with their mother. Today Harris credits her mother, who died in 2009, with being the most important force in her life. Harris particularly admires her mother for instilling her daughters with a thirst for education, a willingness to work hard, and a readiness to act rather than simply to dream. As she describes it in a memoir, "She was the one most responsible for shaping us into the women we would become."[61]

"There was an important role on the inside [of the political system], sitting at the table where decisions were being made. When activists came marching and banging on the doors, I wanted to be on the other side to let them in."[59]

—Kamala Harris

At age twelve, Kamala moved to Montreal, Canada, where her mother had accepted a job at a local hospital. At first Kamala attended a French-language school, but she eventually graduated from an English-speaking high school. Following high school Harris enrolled at Howard University, a historically Black institution in Washington, DC, and the place where Thurgood Marshall attended law school. While in college, Harris was involved in many activities; she was captain of the debate team, for example, and was a member of the school's economics society. She graduated in 1986 with a degree in economics and political science. After graduation, she earned a law degree at the University of California, Berkeley, and became a licensed attorney in 1990.

Prosecutor Harris

Unlike Thurgood Marshall or Stacey Abrams, Harris never practiced law in the private sector. Instead, she moved directly into public service. She began her career as a deputy district attorney in Alameda County, California, where she was born. District attorneys are in charge of prosecuting criminal cases, whether against violent criminals or corporations that are breaking the law. As deputy district attorney Harris assisted in high-profile prosecutions and was responsible for others on her own. Harris did well in this role. As a journalist put it, "She was viewed as an able prosecutor on the way up."[62]

Harris eventually moved on from Alameda County, accepting a post as assistant district attorney for nearby San Francisco in 1998. In this role she focused especially on homicide cases and cases involving sexual assault. Before long, however, she had a disagreement over policy with one of her supervisors, who demoted her. The district attorney at the time, Terence Hallinan, supported the supervisor instead of Harris, allowing the demotion to take place even though he had spoken highly of Harris when she was first hired. Rather than accept the demotion, Harris quit her job and took a position working in the city government of San Francisco.

For some time Harris had thought about running for San Francisco district attorney. In 2002 she decided that she was ready and declared her candidacy for the election the following year. Though she was little known compared to Hallinan, the much higher-profile incumbent, Harris ran a strong campaign. She attacked Hallinan's record, pointing out that he earned convictions on barely half of the serious crimes his office prosecuted, a figure well below the statewide average. She also argued that Hallinan was not doing much to stop gun violence and charged that he did not take domestic abuse seriously. Harris won a surprise victory with 56 percent of the vote, becoming the first African American to serve as San Francisco's district attorney.

Appointments and Controversy

In 1994, while still a prosecutor in Alameda County, Kamala Harris was appointed to a state board in California dealing with unemployment benefits. People who felt they had been wrongly denied these benefits could appeal to the board, which would make a final determination. The position required relatively little time, but it paid quite well. A few months later Harris resigned from this board and was immediately appointed to a similar board, where she and others oversaw insurance payments to hospitals. Again, the position paid well but made few demands on the board members' time.

The fact that Harris served on these boards created some controversy. That was because the appointments were made by California's Speaker of the House, Willie Brown, and Brown and Harris were dating at the time. Many Californians believed that Harris had gotten the board positions based on her relationship with Brown, not on her qualifications. Harris responded that she had worked hard in both roles and asserted that she had been appointed because of her credentials, not the identity of her boyfriend. Nonetheless, many people were not convinced, and the debate over whether Harris belonged on the boards continued for several years.

Harris served two terms as district attorney. She focused on a number of issues while in office. She was a staunch opponent of the death penalty, for example, arguing that life without parole was fairer, more compassionate, and less expensive than execution. At the same time, Harris strengthened penalties for gun violence, hate crimes, and sexual assault. While Harris was willing to prosecute drug cases, moreover, she had little interest in pursuing nonviolent cases involving possession of marijuana. Finally, she developed programs to give young criminals a chance to succeed following their release from prison. Her job as district attorney, Harris writes, was in part "to see and address the causes of crime, not just their consequences, and to shine a light on the inequality and unfairness that lead to injustice."[63]

Attorney General

In 2010, as her second term in the role of district attorney began winding down, Harris started campaigning for another, more powerful post: attorney general of California. The attorney general of a state is the state's highest-ranking prosecutor, responsible for deciding what criminal cases to pursue and how many resources to devote to each. Harris was not given much of a chance of winning the race, but just as she had staged an upset to win the district attorney seat in San Francisco, she won a tight race to become attorney general.

> "[The job of district attorney is] to see and address the causes of crime, not just their consequences, and to shine a light on the inequality and unfairness that lead to injustice."[63]
>
> —Kamala Harris

Harris immediately became involved in a crisis. Many Californians, along with Americans in other states, were unable to pay their mortgages, in part due to unscrupulous tactics used by banks. "Homeowners told me countless stories of personal catastrophe,"[64] Harris recalls. At one point, banks had foreclosed on 2.5 million homeowners nationwide—that is, they had taken back the property and forced the owners to leave due to nonpayment. In a single month in 2011, Harris knew, close to forty thousand homeowners in Los Angeles had lined up outside banks to plead for help. Harris was eager to join a group of attorneys general from other states who were pushing for a fair and equitable settlement to the crisis.

She was not happy, though, when she realized that the other attorneys general had already made a tentative settlement with the banks. The agreement included up to $4 billion in relief for affected homeowners, which Harris thought was far too little. "Compared with the devastation," she writes, "the banks were

48

offering crumbs on the table, nowhere near enough to compensate for the damage they had caused."[65] With help from allies like attorneys general Beau Biden of Delaware and Catherine Cortez Masto of Nevada, Harris pushed for more. During the process she angered many bank presidents—but in the end she got the $4 billion raised to $20 billion.

As attorney general, Harris took positions familiar to those who followed her early career as a prosecutor. In addition to starting new programs to help people recently released from state prison, for example, she continued to be an outspoken opponent of the death penalty and a strong supporter of gun control. During her time as attorney general, Harris also focused on safeguarding abortion rights, protecting the environment, and legalizing same-sex marriage. California had permitted same-sex marriage briefly, but opponents had passed a proposition making

Kamala Harris waves at the crowd at her inauguration for attorney general of California. As attorney general, she was instrumental in negotiating a large settlement with the banking industry for millions of homeowners devastated by the housing crisis created by unethical banking practices.

The wife of the president of the United States—as of 2021, there had never been a president with a husband—is known as the First Lady. Traditionally, the wife of the vice president is referred to as the Second Lady. However, Kamala Harris came into office with a husband, Douglas Emhoff, rather than a wife, and Emhoff is unofficially considered the country's Second Gentleman. He is the first Second Gentleman in the nation's history, and he is also the first Jewish person to be married to a vice president of the United States.

Emhoff is an entertainment lawyer who grew up mainly in New York but moved to the Los Angeles area during high school. When he married Harris in 2014, Emhoff was a divorced father of two children, Cole and Ella. Following Harris's election as vice president, Emhoff stepped down from his law firm; the firm sometimes lobbies government leaders on behalf of its clients, and Emhoff wanted to avoid charges that he was using his influence to reach an outcome favorable to his firm. As of 2021 he was a member of the faculty at Georgetown University's law school in Washington, DC.

it illegal once again. Harris vowed not to enforce the proposition and was overjoyed when a court said it was invalid. "Marriages can resume in California," she told a crowd later that day, "and shall resume in California."[66]

Harris ran for reelection in 2014 and won 57.5 percent of the vote. Popular and effective, she might have remained attorney general for the rest of her career. But in January 2015, just after Harris began her second term, California senator Barbara Boxer announced that she would not run for reelection in 2016. Harris almost immediately announced that she would be joining the Senate race. This time she was neither unknown nor an underdog. She finished first in California's multiparty primary, allowing her to move on to the general election against the second-place finisher, fellow Democrat Loretta Sanchez. Harris won the general election easily and became only the second Black woman ever to serve in the Senate.

The Senate and Beyond

Moving to the Senate did not change Harris's political priorities. She objected strenuously to many of the policies put into place by the new president, Donald Trump, and voted accordingly. She opposed the administration's immigration policies, which she described as racist and cruel, and she voted against many of Trump's nominees for judgeships. She also pressed the House to begin impeachment proceedings against Trump in early 2019, saying, "It is very clear that there is a lot of good evidence"[67] against the president. In the end Trump was impeached twice, and Harris voted to convict in both trials.

Though she was just a first-term senator, Harris announced her candidacy for the 2020 presidential nomination in early 2019. Many Democrats across the country were delighted that she was in the race; within twenty-four hours of her announcement, Harris had raised $1.5 million, an enormous amount for a single day. But after the initial burst of energy, Harris's campaign began to bog down. "At times," notes commentator Perry Bacon Jr., "she struggled to explain her policy stances and her reasons for running for president."[68]

> "At times she struggled to explain her policy stances and her reasons for running for president."[68]
>
> —Perry Bacon Jr., political commentator

Harris also was running against several strong candidates. Former vice president Joe Biden, in particular, was very attractive to Black voters, as was Massachusetts senator Elizabeth Warren to women. The campaign soon ran short of funding, and in November 2019, before the first states chose their delegates, Harris suspended her campaign. However, Biden, the eventual nominee, chose her as his running mate in the summer of 2020. She became the first Black vice presidential candidate of a major party, as well as the first Asian American and only the third woman to hold that distinction.

The 2020 presidential campaign was bitter. Trump engaged in multiple verbal assaults against Harris, calling her "this monster" and "totally unlikeable."[69] Harris responded by calling Trump's remarks childish and unpresidential. She and Biden put forward their vision of America while attacking Trump's record. The election was close, and it took time for all the votes to be counted. But within a week Biden and Harris were declared the winners by a margin of 306 to 232 in the electoral college. Trump and his allies brought dozens of lawsuits designed to overturn the election, and some of his followers broke into the Capitol on January 6, 2021, in an attempt to invalidate the results. But their efforts did not succeed. On January 20 Biden and Harris were sworn into office.

Vice presidents, as a rule, do not have many responsibilities, but Harris began her time in office by swearing in three new senators: Alex Padilla, her replacement in California, and the two new Georgia senators, Jon Ossoff and Raphael Warnock. The vice president also serves as president of the Senate, which enables the person in that role to cast tie-breaking votes. Given that the Senate is evenly divided between Democrats and Republicans, Harris has had several opportunities to do so. In her first six months, she cast seven tie-breaking votes, including one that ensured the passage of an important stimulus act.

In her early days of office, Harris has also played an important role in supporting the Biden administration's political agenda. In June 2021, for instance, she made a trip to Central America to address increased migration from that region to the United States. "I want to be clear to folks in the region who are thinking of making that dangerous trek to the United States–Mexico border: Do not come,"[70] she said in a press conference. It will be interesting to see what Harris does in the rest of her time as vice president—and what she has in mind once her term in office is over.

Introduction: Activism and Government

1. Quoted in Lottie L. Joiner, "Remembering Civil Rights Heroine Fannie Lou Hamer," Daily Beast, September 2, 2014. www.thedailybeast.com.
2. Quoted in *USA Today*, "Shirley Chisholm, First Black Woman Elected to Congress, Dies," January 2, 2005. https://usatoday30.usatoday.com.

Chapter One
Thurgood Marshall: Lawyer and Supreme Court Justice

3. Quoted in Charles Moritz, ed., *Current Biography Yearbook 1989*. New York: Wilson, 1989, p. 378.
4. Quoted in Randy Dotinga, "'Showdown' Tells How Strom Thurmond Tried to Keep Thurgood Marshall Off the Supreme Court," *Christian Science Monitor*, October 29, 2015. www.csmonitor.com.
5. Quoted in Walter McClintock, ed., *Current Biography Yearbook 1954*. New York: Wilson, 1954, p. 441.
6. Quoted in Legal Information Institute, "14th Amendment." www.law.cornell.edu.
7. Quoted in NAACP Legal Defense and Educational Fund, "A Revealing Experiment: *Brown v. Board* and 'the Doll Test,'" 2021. www.naacpldf.org.
8. Quoted in PBS, "Beyond Brown: Full History," 2004. www.pbs.org.
9. Quoted in Moritz, *Current Biography Yearbook 1989*, p. 379.
10. Quoted in Lincoln Caplan, "The Political Solicitor General," *Harvard Magazine*, September/October 2018. www.harvardmagazine.com.
11. Quoted in Andrew Glass, "LBJ Nominates Thurgood Marshall to Supreme Court, June 13, 1967," Politico, June 13, 2018. www.politico.com.
12. Quoted in Nat Hentoff, "The Machinery of Death Grinds On," *Washington Post*, April 12, 1997. www.washingtonpost.com.
13. Quoted in Lincoln Caplan, "Thurgood Marshall and the Need for Affirmative Action," *New Yorker*, December 9, 2015. www.newyorker.com.

14. Quoted in Joan Biskupic, "Thurgood Marshall, Retired Justice, Dies," *Washington Post*, January 25, 1993. www.washingtonpost.com.

Chapter Two
John Lewis: Activist and US Representative

15. Quoted in Jon Meacham, *His Truth Is Marching On*. New York: Random House, 2020, p. 24.
16. John Lewis, *Across That Bridge*. New York: Hachette, 2012, p. 95.
17. Quoted in Meacham, *His Truth Is Marching On*, pp. 30–31.
18. Quoted in Lewis, *Across That Bridge*, p. 80.
19. Quoted in Vann R. Newkirk II, "How Martin Luther King Jr. Recruited John Lewis," *The Atlantic*, February 2018. www.theatlantic.com.
20. Quoted in Jennifer Haberkorn, "John Lewis, Civil Rights Icon and Longtime Congressman, Dies," *Los Angeles Times*, July 17, 2020. www.latimes.com.
21. Quoted in Meacham, *His Truth Is Marching On*, p. 72.
22. Quoted in Haberkorn, "John Lewis, Civil Rights Icon and Longtime Congressman, Dies."
23. Dudley Clendinen, "Ex-colleague Upsets Julian Bond in Atlanta Congressional Runoff," *New York Times*, September 3, 1986. www.nytimes.com.
24. Quoted in Haberkorn, "John Lewis, Civil Rights Icon and Longtime Congressman, Dies."
25. Quoted in Tamar Hallerman, "John Lewis Saw in Gay Rights a Movement like Civil Rights," *Atlanta Journal-Constitution*, July 17, 2020. www.ajc.com.
26. Quoted in Javier Panzar, "Rep. John Lewis Speaks Out Against Trump's Divisive Rhetoric During L.A. Visit," *Los Angeles Times*, January 23, 2016. www.latimes.com.
27. Quoted in Jeff Zeleny and Patrick Healy, "Black Leader, a Clinton Ally, Tilts to Obama," *New York Times*, February 15, 2008. www.nytimes.com.
28. Quoted in Paul LeBlanc and Elizabeth Cohen, "Civil Rights Icon Rep. John Lewis Announces He Has Stage 4 Pancreatic Cancer," CNN, December 30, 2019. www.cnn.com.
29. Quoted in Meacham, *His Truth Is Marching On*, p. 249.

Chapter Three
Barack Obama: US President

30. John Moore, "Obama's Victory Elates Friends of Shadow Theatre," *Denver (CO) Post*, November 6, 2008. www.denverpost.com.
31. Barack Obama, *Dreams from My Father*. New York: Times Books, 1995, p. 60.

32. Quoted in Oprah.com, "Keeping Hope Alive," October 18, 2006. www.oprah.com.
33. Barack Obama, "Barack Obama: A Letter to My Daughters," *Parade*, January 18, 2009. https://parade.com.
34. Quoted in John Sepulvado, "Obama's 'Overnight Success' in 2004 Was a Year in the Making," OPB, May 19, 2016. www.opb.org.
35. Quoted in *Chicago Tribune*, "Obama to Give Keynote Address," July 15, 2004. www.chicagotribune.com.
36. Quoted in David Bernstein, "The Speech," *Chicago*, May 27, 2009. www.chicagomag.com.
37. Barack Obama, "Barack Obama's Remarks to the National Convention," *New York Times*, July 27, 2004. www.nytimes.com.
38. Quoted in Audie Cornish, "Rare National Buzz Tipped Obama's Decision to Run," NPR, November 19, 2007. www.npr.org.
39. Barack Obama, "Transcript: Barack Obama's Acceptance Speech," NPR, August 28, 2008. www.npr.org.
40. Barack Obama, "Statement by the President on the School Shooting in Newtown, CT," White House, December 14, 2012. https://obamawhitehouse.archives.gov.
41. Quoted in Glenn Kessler, "When Did McConnell Say He Wanted to Make Obama a 'One-Term President'?," *Washington Post*, September 24, 2012. www.washingtonpost.com.
42. Quoted in BBC, "DNC 2020: Obama Blasts Trump's 'Reality Show' Presidency," August 20, 2020. www.bbc.com.
43. Obama Foundation, "Our Mission." www.obama.org.

Chapter Four
Stacey Abrams: Voting Rights Activist

44. Molly Ball, "Stacey Abrams Could Become America's First Black Female Governor—If She Can Turn Georgia Blue," *Time*, July 26, 2018. https://time.com.
45. Quoted in Ball, "Stacey Abrams Could Become America's First Black Female Governor—If She Can Turn Georgia Blue."
46. Stacey Abrams, *Lead from the Outside*. New York, Picador, 2018, p. 8.
47. Quoted in Amelia Poor, "One-on-One with Stacey Abrams," *Scholastic Kids*, May 17, 2019. https://kpcnotebook.scholastic.com.
48. Abrams, *Lead from the Outside*, p. 10.
49. Quoted in Martha S. Jones, *Vanguard*. New York: Basic Books, 2020, p. 276.
50. Abrams, *Lead from the Outside*, p. 23.
51. Abrams, *Lead from the Outside*, pp. 42–43.
52. Ball, "Stacey Abrams Could Become America's First Black Female Governor—If She Can Turn Georgia Blue."

53. Alan Judd, "Georgia's Strict Laws Lead to Large Purge of Voters," *Atlanta Journal-Constitution*, October 27, 2018. www.ajc.com.

54. Quoted in Ben Nadler, "Voting Rights Become a Flashpoint in Georgia Governor's Race," AP News, October 29, 2018. https://apnews.com.

55. Quoted in James Arkin, "Stacey Abrams Won't Run for Senate," Politico, April 30, 2019. www.politico.com.

56. Quoted in AP News, "Abrams Brings Fair Fight 2020 to Georgia," August 17, 2019. https://apnews.com.

57. Ankita Rao et al., "How Georgia's Senate Runoffs Could Finally Hand Stacey Abrams Her Victory," *The Guardian* (Manchester, UK), November 9, 2020. www.theguardian.com.

58. Quoted in Quint Forgey, "Stacey Abrams Says She'll Be President by 2040," Politico, January 31, 2020. www.politico.com.

Chapter Five
Kamala Harris: US Vice President

59. Kamala Harris, *The Truths We Hold*. New York: Penguin, 2019, p. 25.

60. Quoted in Chevaz Clarke, "Get to Know Kamala Harris' Family," CBS News, January 20, 2021. www.cbsnews.com.

61. Harris, *The Truths We Hold*, p. 6.

62. Dan Morain, "2 More Brown Associates Get Well-Paid Posts," *Los Angeles Times*, November 29, 1994. www.latimes.com.

63. Quoted in German Lopez, "Kamala Harris's Controversial Record on Criminal Justice, Explained," Vox, January 23, 2019. www.vox.com.

64. Harris, *The Truths We Hold*, p. 80.

65. Harris, *The Truths We Hold*, p. 93.

66. Quoted in Anne Almendrala, "Kamala Harris on Prop 8 Decision: Same-Sex Marriages in California Should Begin Immediately," HuffPost, June 27, 2013. www.huffpost.com.

67. Quoted in Felicia Sonmez and Chelsea Janes, "Sen. Kamala Harris Says She Supports Impeaching Trump," *Washington Post*, April 22, 2019. www.washingtonpost.com.

68. Perry Bacon Jr., "Why Kamala Harris's Campaign Failed," FiveThirtyEight, December 3, 2019. https://fivethirtyeight.com.

69. Quoted in Juana Summers, "Trump Calls Harris a 'Monster,' Reviving a Pattern of Attacking Women of Color," NPR, October 9, 2020. www.npr.org.

70. Quoted in Sabrina Rodriguez, "Harris' Blunt Message in Guatemala: 'Do Not Come' to U.S.," Politico, June 7, 2021. www.politico.com.

FOR FURTHER RESEARCH

Books

Stacey Abrams, *Lead from the Outside*. New York, Picador, 2018.

Spencer R. Crew, *Thurgood Marshall: A Life in American History*. Santa Barbara, CA: ABC-CLIO, 2019.

Mark Greenberg and David Tait, *Obama*. New York: Sterling, 2020.

Kamala Harris, *The Truths We Hold*. New York: Penguin, 2019.

John Lewis and Kabir Sehgal, *Carry On: Reflections for a New Generation*. New York: Hachette, 2021.

Internet Sources

Molly Ball, "Stacey Abrams Could Become America's First Black Female Governor—If She Can Turn Georgia Blue," *Time*, July 26, 2018. https://time.com.

Joan Biskupic, "Thurgood Marshall, Retired Justice, Dies," *Washington Post*, January 25, 1993. www.washingtonpost.com.

Lisa Lerer and Sydney Ember, "Kamala Harris Makes History as First Woman and Woman of Color as Vice President," *New York Times*, November 7, 2020. www.nytimes.com.

Vann R. Newkirk II, "How Martin Luther King Jr. Recruited John Lewis," *The Atlantic*, February 2018. www.theatlantic.com.

Barack Obama, "Barack Obama's Remarks to the National Convention," *New York Times*, July 27, 2004. www.nytimes.com.

Websites

Civil Rights Digital Library
http://crdl.usg.edu
This website has documents, videos, and other material related to the civil rights movement and the struggle for racial equality. It includes resources aimed at teachers, students, and researchers.

Fair Fight Action

www.fairfight.com

Fair Fight Action was founded by Stacey Abrams to advocate for fair elections and to uphold the right to vote. The website gives information about the activities of the organization, along with providing educational materials and news reports related to voting rights.

The Office of Barack and Michelle Obama

www.barackobama.com

This site provides biographical background for Barack Obama and his wife, Michelle. It also includes information about the Obama Foundation and other projects the two are involved in.

The White House: Kamala Harris: Vice President

www.whitehouse.gov/administration/vice-president-harris

In addition to giving biographical information about Harris, this website describes some of her official activities in her capacity as vice president of the United States.

INDEX

PICTURE CREDITS

ABOUT THE AUTHOR

Stephen Currie is the author of several dozen books for young people, many of them for ReferencePoint Press. He has also taught at grade levels ranging from kindergarten to college. He lives with his family in New York's Hudson Valley.